sending you all my love and
lots of hugs & prayers. (Psalm 139)

Jeni & Phil ♡

Alyssa (Hawkins) Cole

Oct. 22, 2020

Beside Still Waters

Refreshing Moments to Restore Your Soul

PAINTINGS BY

Darrell Bush

HARVEST HOUSE PUBLISHERS

EUGENE, OREGON

Beside Still Waters

Text Copyright © 2010 by Hope Lyda
Artwork Copyright © 2010 by Darrell Bush

Published by Harvest House Publishers
Eugene, Oregon 97402
www.harvesthousepublishers.com

ISBN 978-0-7369-2632-4

Artwork designs are reproduced under license from © 2010 by Darrell Bush, courtesy of MHS Licensing, and may not be reproduced without permission.

Design and production by Garborg Design Works, Savage, Minnesota

Harvest House Publishers has made every effort to trace the ownership of all poems and quotes. In the event of a question arising from the use of a poem or quote, we regret any error made and will be pleased to make the necessary correction in future editions of this book.

Printed in China

10 11 12 13 14 15 16 / LP / 10 9 8 7 6 5 4 3 2

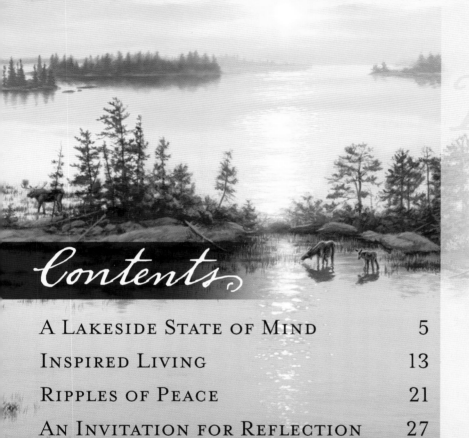

Contents

I remember a hundred lovely lakes, and recall the fragrant breath of pine and fir and cedar and poplar trees. The trail has strung upon it, as upon a thread of silk, opalescent dawns and saffron sunsets. It has given me blessed release from care and worry and the troubled thinking of our modern day. It has been a return to the primitive and the peaceful.

HAMLIN GARLAND

A Lakeside State of Mind

How were you introduced to the lakeside state of mind? Fishing the pristine lakes of the Midwest? Exploring trail-lined gems in the Pacific Northwest? Boating on wide-open expanses of water in the South? Maybe a magazine photo of a solitary Adirondack chair facing a clear blue lake captured your attention and filled your dreams.

The lakeside state of mind welcomes solitude and moments of silence. It notices the magic of dusk and the miracle of the dawn. It nurtures beauty and appreciates every sweet moment of life. It relaxes the shoulders, inspires deep breathing, and leads you to not only ponder life but also to live it—fully and vibrantly!

Have you flung your body from a tire swing into the glassy surface at your favorite waterhole? Have you splashed cold water on your face after a long day at work? Did you ever delight in the buoyancy of water at your local pool? Do you savor the comfort and renewal of a long bath? These are all invigorating and restorative gifts of the lakeside state of mind. Dive in.

Better than any argument is to rise at dawn and pick dew-wet red berries in a cup.

WENDELL BERRY

5

Savor the Pleasures

PERFECT CATCH PARMESAN CATFISH

½ cup dry bread crumbs
¼ cup grated Parmesan cheese
2 tablespoons chopped fresh parsley
½ teaspoon paprika
¼ teaspoon dried oregano
¼ teaspoon dried basil leaves
a pinch of black pepper
1 pound skinless catfish fillets
⅓ cup low fat milk
2 teaspoons vegetable oil

Mix together bread crumbs, cheese, and seasonings. Dip each fillet in milk and then roll in dry mixture. Place fish in a baking dish coated with nonstick cooking spray and then drizzle oil over the fillets. Bake at 450 degrees for 8 to 10 minutes or until fish flakes easily when tested with a fork. Makes 2 servings.

We do not see nature with our eyes, but with our understandings and our hearts.

WILLIAM HAZLITT

There is no greatness
where there is not simplicity.

Leo Tolstoy

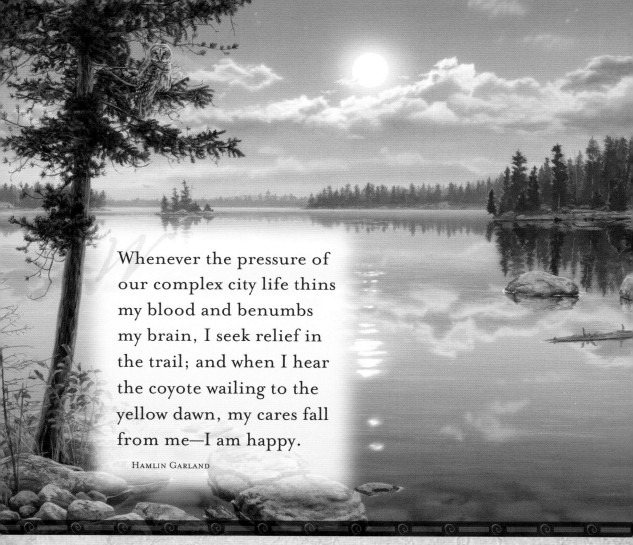

Whenever the pressure of our complex city life thins my blood and benumbs my brain, I seek relief in the trail; and when I hear the coyote wailing to the yellow dawn, my cares fall from me—I am happy.

HAMLIN GARLAND

A lake carries you into recesses of

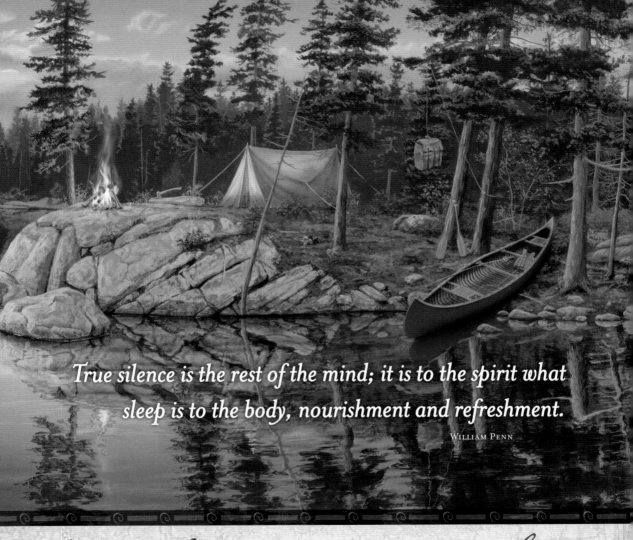

True silence is the rest of the mind; it is to the spirit what sleep is to the body, nourishment and refreshment.

WILLIAM PENN

feeling otherwise impenetrable.

WILLIAM WORDSWORTH

You must not know too much, or be too precise or scientific about birds and trees and flowers and watercraft; a certain free margin, and even vagueness—perhaps ignorance, credulity—helps your enjoyment of these things.

<small>WALT WHITMAN</small>

There is one piece of advice, in a life of study, which I think no one will object to; and that is, every now and then to be completely idle—to do nothing at all.

<small>SYDNEY SMITH</small>

Inspired Living

The inspiration of the glassy lake or the gently flowing river follows you wherever you go. You can adopt a pared-down, simple style at work and home—or delight in the joy of recreation as you embrace an active life. Welcoming a relaxed, meditative lifestyle all year round is also a way to enjoy the pleasures of waterfront living. But when the bumper sticker on the vehicle ahead of you reads "My other car is a boat" and a deep sense of longing kicks in, it might be time to plan your next escape to your personal hideaway. Close your eyes and imagine it!

When you arrive at the water's edge, your heart expands with joy and anticipation. You hear your winged neighbors chatter in the treetops and suspect they're discussing how long you've been away. The mental clutter of the busy life clears from your head, and the urge to kick off your shoes must be obeyed. Whether you slip your feet into soothing waters, roomy slippers, or yellow rain boots, you wonder why you even own a pair of restrictive shoes.

The gentle sounds of the water welcome you back. You feel at home, beloved, and comfortable in your own skin. You breathe in deeply and let out a sigh as your soul realizes a great truth: This is what it's like to spend time with God.

Besides the noble art of getting things done, there is a nobler art of leaving things undone. The wisdom of life consists in the elimination of nonessentials.

LIN YUTANG

There is nothing that God hath established in a constant course of nature, and which therefore is done every day, but would seem a Miracle, and exercise our admiration, if it were done but once.

JOHN DONNE

In all things of nature there is something

of the marvelous.

ARISTOTLE

Savor the Pleasures

EARLY RISER BLUEBERRY PANCAKES

½ cup milk
2 tablespoons melted butter or margarine
1 large egg
1 cup all-purpose flour
2 teaspoons baking powder
2 teaspoons sugar
¾ to 1 cup blueberries
⅓ cup chopped pecans (or nuts of choice)

Combine wet ingredients (milk, melted butter, and egg) and mix well. Add sifted flour, baking powder, and sugar to the wet ingredients. Stir just enough to dampen the flour. If batter is too thick, add a little more milk. Gently add the blueberries and pecans. Place a skillet over medium heat. When hot, coat skillet lightly with oil and spoon batter in ⅓-cup portions onto the skillet. When pancakes fluff up and bubbles form on the surface, flip the pancakes and brown on the other side. Makes 4 servings.

15

A person should go out on the water on a fine day to a small distance from a beautiful coast, if he would see Nature really smile. Never does she look so delightful, as when the sun is brightly reflected by the water, while the waves are gently rippling, and the prospect receives life and animation from the glancing transit of an occasional row-boat, and the quieter motion of a few small vessels.

Augustus William Hare and Julius Charles Hare

THE RICHNESS

Nature is the art of God.

THOMAS BROWNE

CHIEVE COMES FROM NATURE, THE SOURCE OF MY INSPIRATION.

CLAUDE MONET

The glow of inspiration warms us; this holy rapture springs from the seeds of the Divine mind sown in man.

OVID

BE PRAISED, MY LORD, THROUGH SISTER WATER;
SHE IS VERY USEFUL, AND HUMBLE, AND PRECIOUS, AND PURE.

ST. FRANCIS OF ASSISI

Innumerable as the stars of night,
Or stars of morning, dewdrops which the sun
Impearls on every leaf and every flower.

JOHN MILTON, FROM *PARADISE LOST*

Ripples of Peace

"Let There Be Peace on Earth" could serve as a year-round anthem for those who dwell a stone's throw from the water's edge. They are blessed in every season with the tranquility and serenity of nature. Peace is witnessed daily in the harmony between the flora and fauna. Peace is felt in the strength of a thick grove of trees and the open freedom of a lush meadow. It is experienced through the generosity of interdependent neighbors. Peace is cultivated in times of silence. It leads the way along meandering, tree-lined roads that lead to a new day's hope around the next bend.

This peace ripples throughout every area of life for all who are fortunate enough to be born with the rhythm of the water in their hearts—no matter where they live. Are you one of these lucky people? When you survey the tranquility of Creation's glory, do you believe that peace on earth can begin with you in this moment of wonder? Let such peace reside in your heart!

Adopt the pace of nature: her secret is patience.

Ralph Waldo Emerson

Savor the Pleasures

PESTO TROUT

1 large lake trout fillet
Pesto sauce
2 tablespoons lime or lemon juice
2 to 3 tablespoons olive oil

Coat the thawed or fresh fillet with pesto. Add olive oil to a skillet and place over medium heat. When hot, put fillet meat side down into the pan. Allow to cook for 3 minutes until nicely browned. Flip the fillet and add the citrus juice and a splash of water to the skillet and cover. Reduce heat slightly and allow the trout to cook for another 3 to 4 minutes or until the fish flakes easily and detaches from the skin cleanly. Makes 2 servings.

of grace, is a mere hook without the bait.

CHARLES MAURICE DE TALLEYRAND-PERIGORD

The lakes are something which you are unprepared for; they lie up so high, exposed to the light, and the forest is diminished to a fine fringe on their edges, with here and there a blue mountain, like amethyst jewels set around some jewel of the first water—so anterior, so superior, to all the changes that are to take place on their shores, even now civil and refined, and fair as they can ever be.

HENRY DAVID THOREAU

You are my hiding place;
you will protect me from trouble
and surround me with songs of deliverance.

PSALM 32:7

24

FIRST KEEP THE PEACE WITHIN YOURSELF,
THEN YOU CAN ALSO BRING PEACE TO OTHERS.

THOMAS A KEMPIS

A lonely lake, a lonely shore,
A lone pine leaning on the moon;
All night the water-beating wings
Of a solitary loon.

LEW SARETT

An Invitation for Reflection

In the light of a new dawn, the lake's still surface mirrors the shifting clouds, the rising sun. This early hour beckons you to explore the calm. Grabbing a fleece jacket and a knit cap to ease the morning chill, you walk instinctively to the head of the trail and start a slight downward stroll.

The path, familiar and welcoming, has been carved out of the ferns, cattails, and occasional nettles from many treks down to the water. As you walk, your mind also follows a well-worn trail. This is your personal time of reflection and prayer. It is second nature to lift up praises when surrounded by the sights and sounds of the lake. And when your heart is weary, this is a journey of prayers and petitions; a walk to gather strength and peace.

Each step takes you closer to the shore and deeper into the joy of solitude. At your favorite spot, you can crouch down low to the water's edge and see into its depths. When the wind dies down and the water returns to stillness, you notice your image reflected in the watery surface. You smile and wave to the lucky one who gets to spend their first waking moments alone with their Creator, their thoughts, and the peace of the water.

A lake is the landscape's most beautiful and expressive feature. It is earth's eye; looking into which the beholder measures the depth of his own nature.

HENRY DAVID THOREAU

27

To be glad of life because it gives you the chance to love and to work and to play and to look up at the stars, to be satisfied with your possessions but not contented with yourself until you have made the best of them, to despise nothing in the world except falsehood and meanness and to fear nothing except cowardice, to be governed by your admirations rather than by your disgusts, to covet nothing that is your neighbor's except his kindness of heart and gentleness of manners, to think seldom of your enemies, often of your friends...and to spend as much time as you can, with body and with spirit, in God's out-of-doors, these are little guideposts on the footpath to peace.

HENRY VAN DYKE

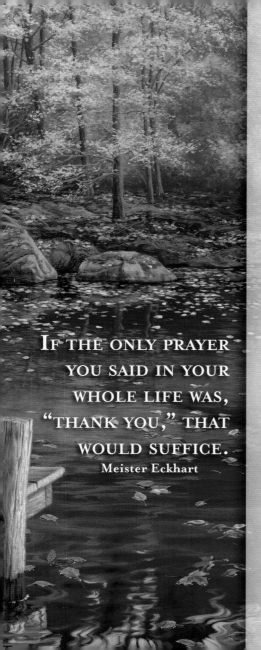

IF THE ONLY PRAYER
YOU SAID IN YOUR
WHOLE LIFE WAS,
"THANK YOU," THAT
WOULD SUFFICE.
Meister Eckhart

Savor the Pleasures
COZY AND DELICIOUS COCOA

⅓ cup unsweetened cocoa powder
¾ cup white sugar
1 to 2 pinches salt
⅓ cup boiling water
3½ cups milk
¾ teaspoon vanilla extract
½ cup half-and-half cream

Combine cocoa, sugar, and salt in a saucepan. Add the boiling water. While stirring, bring this mixture to an easy boil. Simmer and stir for another couple of minutes, making sure that it does not scorch. Stir in the milk and heat until very hot but not boiling. Remove from heat and add the vanilla extract. Promptly pour into mugs and add half-and-half cream to each mug to adjust the temperature. Makes 4 servings.

I love to think of nature as an unlimited broadcasting station, through which God speaks to us every hour, if we will only tune in.

GEORGE WASHINGTON CARVER

It is in deep solitude that I find the gentleness with which I can truly love my brothers. The more solitary I am the more affection I have for them... Solitude and silence teach me to love my brothers for what they are, not for what they say.

THOMAS MERTON

And lo! in a flash of crimson splendor, with blazing scarlet clouds running before his chariot, and heralding his majestic approach, God's sun rises upon the world.

WILLIAM MAKEPEACE THACKERAY

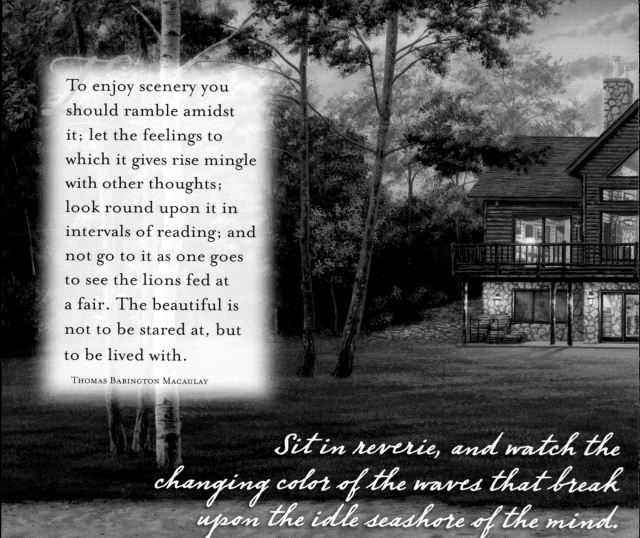

To enjoy scenery you should ramble amidst it; let the feelings to which it gives rise mingle with other thoughts; look round upon it in intervals of reading; and not go to it as one goes to see the lions fed at a fair. The beautiful is not to be stared at, but to be lived with.

THOMAS BABINGTON MACAULAY

Sit in reverie, and watch the changing color of the waves that break upon the idle seashore of the mind.

HENRY WADSWORTH LONGFELLOW

Take almost any path you please, and ten to one it carries you down in a dale, and leaves you there by a pool in the stream. There is magic in it.

HERMAN MELVILLE, FROM *MOBY DICK*

Gifts of Abundance

"They're really biting today!" a neighbor calls out from behind the foliage of a low-hanging limb of a maple tree. He is hidden out of view, but you don't need to see him or the fresh water trout dangling at the end of his line to know that he's celebrating the harvest of the lake. And it isn't just during fishing season that a lake-goer gets to indulge in the bounty of the water. Daily, the lake makes its offering. There is delight in a pail of ripe blackberries plucked from overgrown bushes along the trail or a cluster of smooth rocks collected along the shore. There are the night sounds of the loons and the frogs that lull even insomniacs to slumber.

The most abundant offerings of the lake are the special memories made in every season, in every setting. In winter, families gather in snow-wrapped cabins for holiday cheer and personalized mugs of hot cocoa. And when temperatures rise, friends make the lake a destination for canoe races and the backdrop for barbeques.

In every season of life, we can act and speak from a grateful heart. As we find ways to give, rather than to receive, we discover the meaning and joy of abundance.

Any one thing in the creation is sufficient to demonstrate a Providence to a humble and grateful mind.

EPICTETUS

Savor the Pleasures

BREADED, BOUNTIFUL BASS

2 eggs, lightly beaten
4 tablespoons lime juice (or lemon)
1 pound fish fillets
cracker crumbs
butter

Combine eggs and lime juice. Dip the fillets in this mixture. Next, coat the fillets in the cracker crumbs. Add butter to a skillet and place over medium heat. When hot, place fillets into the pan. Allow to cook for 3 minutes until nicely browned. Flip fillets and brown other side until the fish flakes easily when tested with a fork. To serve, add slices of lime for presentation and an extra dash of flavor. Makes 4 servings.

WATER IS THE DRIVER OF NATURE.

LEONARDO DA VINCI

God writes the
gospel not in
the Bible alone,
but on trees
and flowers
and clouds
and stars.

MARTIN LUTHER

The underlying attraction of the movement
of water and sand is biological. If we look
more deeply we can see it as the basis of
an abstract idea linking ourselves with the
limitless mechanics of the universe.

SIR GEOFFREY JELLICOE

More than half the intense enjoyment of fly-fishing is derived from the beautiful surroundings, the satisfaction felt from being in the open air, the new lease of life secured thereby, and the many, many pleasant recollections of all one has seen, heard, and done.

CHARLES ORVIS

> *Smooth runs the water where the brook is deep.*
>
> WILLIAM SHAKESPEARE

This is the meeting place where God has set his bounds. Here is enough, at last, for eye and thought, restful and satisfying and illimitable. Here rest is sweet, and the picture of it goes with us on our homeward way, more lasting in memory than the sunset on the meadows or the lingering light across the silent stream.

ISAAC OGDEN RANKIN

39

Daily Renewal

Just like the gifts of life, the gifts of the quiet waters are plentiful when you take time to notice. Water is a life source for plants, animals, and people. Even the most serene body of water is an active place of growth, renewal, and bounty. Plants along the lake's muddied bottom or the lazy river's rocky bank provide nutrients for fish and deer and woodland creatures. Those lucky enough to experience waterfront living also receive sustenance. It is a source of physical nourishment and more importantly, it is a source of spiritual nourishment. When we stand on the bow of a boat or perch on the rocks that outline the shore, the view connects us to our Creator. Examining this display of beauty allows us to see, with keener vision, the beauty of an intimate God.

We are born with a thirst and hunger for renewal. We hope for new beginnings. Life on the water's edge reminds us of our truest longings and of the fulfiller of these longings. Whether we are personally in search of healing, faith, or waves of hopefulness, we can come to the source of life and be transformed.

I go to nature to be soothed and healed, and to have my senses put in order.

JOHN BURROUGHS

41

Savor the Pleasures

CRIMSON CRISP

1 quart fresh raspberries
⅓ cup granulated sugar
¼ cup butter, softened
¾ cup rolled oats
⅓ cup all-purpose flour
⅓ cup brown sugar

Preheat oven to 350 degrees. Pour the fresh raspberries in the bottom of a 9-inch square baking pan. Sprinkle sugar over the berries. In a separate bowl, blend together the butter, oats, flour, and brown sugar until it becomes a coarse mixture. Sprinkle this mixture over the berries. Bake about 30 minutes or until lightly golden brown. Serve hot, either solo or with a scoop of vanilla ice cream. Makes 4 to 6 servings.

Earth has not anything to show more fair:
Dull would he be of soul who could pass by
A sight so touching in its majesty.

WILLIAM WORDSWORTH

A thing of beauty is a joy forever.

JOHN KEATS

As the deer pants for streams of water,
so my soul pants for you, O God.
My soul thirsts for God, for the living God.

PSALM 42:1-2

Away up in the very heart of Maine there is a mighty lake among the mountains. It is reached after a journey of many hours from the place where you "go in." That is the phrase of the country, and when you have once "gone in," you know why it is not correct to say that you have gone *through* the woods, or, simply, *to* your destination. You find that you have plunged into a new world—a world that has nothing in common with the world that you live in; a world of wild, solemn, desolate grandeur, a world of space and silence; a world that oppresses your soul—and charms you irresistibly. And after you have once "come out" of that world, there will be times, to the day of your death, when you will be homesick for it, and will long with a childlike longing to go back to it.

H.C. BUNNER

NEVER DOES NATURE SAY ONE THING AND WISDOM ANOTHER.

Juvenal

THE POETRY OF THE
EARTH IS NEVER DEAD.

JOHN KEATS

Your sacred space is where you can

I hear lake water lapping with low sounds by the shore...
I hear it in the deep heart's core.

WILLIAM BUTLER YEATS

find yourself again and again.

JOSEPH CAMPBELL

My heart is awed within me when I think
Of the great miracle that still goes on,
In silence, round me—the perpetual work
Of thy creation, finished, yet renewed
Forever. Written on thy works I read
The lesson of thy own eternity.

WILLIAM CULLEN BRYANT